CLARINET DUETS

SHARE THE LEAD

*Now you can play clarinet
duets on eight specially recorded
arrangements*

CHART HITS

**International
MUSIC
Publications**

International Music Publications Limited
Griffin House 161 Hammersmith Road London W6 8BS England

Series Editor: Sadie Cook

Music arrangements: Jerry Lanning

Editorial, production and recording: Artemis Music Limited

Design and production: Space DPS Limited

Published 2000

International
MUSIC
Publications

© International Music Publications Limited
Griffin House 161 Hammersmith Road London W6 8BS England

International Music Publications Limited

England: Griffin House
                  161 Hammersmith Road
                  London W6 8BS

Germany: Marstallstr. 8
                  D-80539 München

Denmark: Danmusik
                  Vognmagergade 7
                  DK1120 Copenhagen K

Carisch

Italy: Nuova Carisch Srl
                  Via Campania 12
                  20098 San Giuliano Milanese
                  Milano

Spain: Nueva Carisch España
                  Magallanes, 25
                  28015 Madrid

France: Carisch Musicom
                  25, Rue d'Hauteville
                  75010 Paris

In the Book...

On the CD...

Track **1**   Tuning tones (A concert)

Dancing Queen
Track **2**   Full version
Track **3**   Part two plus backing track
Track **4**   Part one plus backing track
Track **5**   Backing track

Love's Got A Hold On My Heart
Track **6**   Full version
Track **7**   Part two plus backing track
Track **8**   Part one plus backing track
Track **9**   Backing track

Flying Without Wings
Track **10**   Full version
Track **11**   Part two plus backing track
Track **12**   Part one plus backing track
Track **13**   Backing track

How Do I Live
Track **14**   Full version
Track **15**   Part two plus backing track
Track **16**   Part one plus backing track
Track **17**   Backing track

My Heart Will Go On
Track **18**   Full version
Track **19**   Part two plus backing track
Track **20**   Part one plus backing track
Track **21**   Backing track

More Than Words
Track **22**   Full version
Track **23**   Part two plus backing track
Track **24**   Part one plus backing track
Track **25**   Backing track

When You Say Nothing At All
Track **26**   Full version
Track **27**   Part two plus backing track
Track **28**   Part one plus backing track
Track **29**   Backing track

You Needed Me
Track **30**   Full version
Track **31**   Part two plus backing track
Track **32**   Part one plus backing track
Track **33**   Backing track

Introduction

Welcome to **Share The Lead: Chart Hits**, part of an instrumental series that provides both young and not-so-young players with well-known songs and tunes as duets. You will find that both parts have been arranged in a way that ensures playing either part is interesting and musically satisfying – so don't be surprised to find that part two occasionally has the melody!

All eight pieces have been carefully selected and arranged at an easy level to provide fun material for today's clarinettists, and you will also find that the arrangements can be used with the other instruments in the series - flute, violin and alto saxophone.

The professionally recorded backing CD allows you to hear each song in four different ways:
• a complete demonstration performance with both duet parts being played over the backing
• part two and the backing, so you can play along on part one
• part one and the backing, so you can play along on part two
• backing only, so you and another player can **Share The Lead**

Wherever possible we have simplified the more tricky rhythms, but if you are in any doubt listen to the complete performance tracks and follow the style of the players. Also, we have kept marks of expression to a minimum, but feel free to experiment with these.

Above all, have fun and enjoy the experience of making music together.

6

Dancing Queen

Demonstration Backing for part 1

Backing for part 2 Backing for both parts

Words and Music by Benny Andersson,
Stig Anderson and Björn Ulvaeus

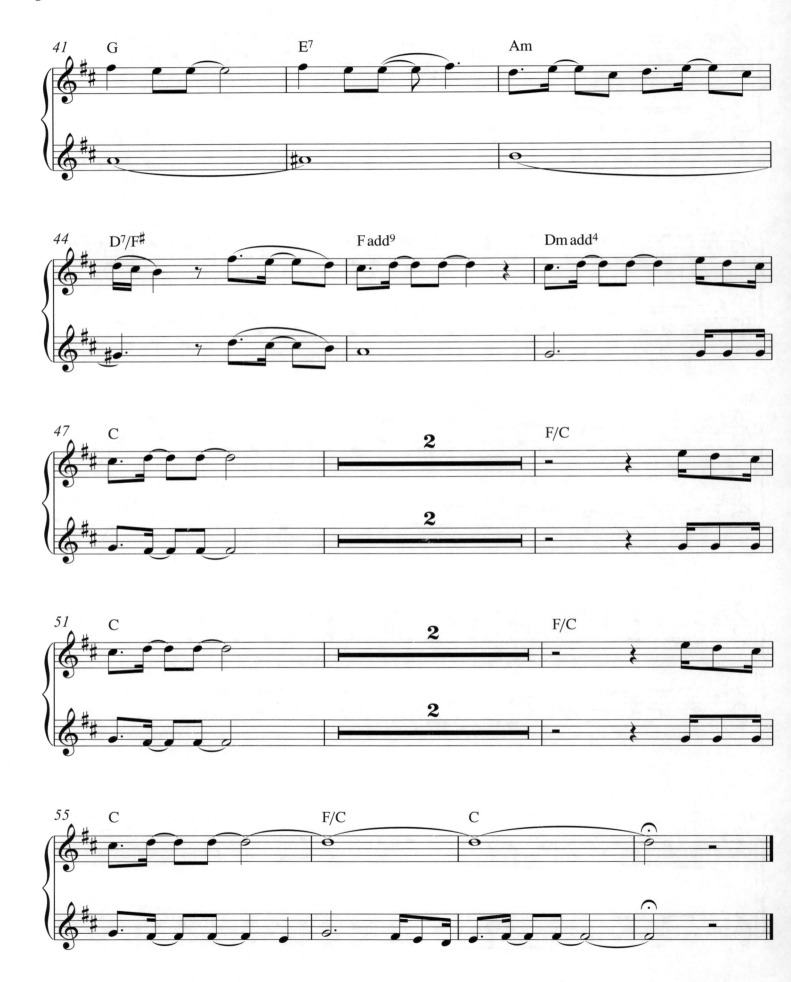

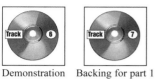

Love's Got A Hold
On My Heart

Demonstration   Backing for part 1

Backing for part 2   Backing for both parts

Words and Music by
Andrew Frampton and Pete Waterman

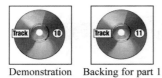

Demonstration   Backing for part 1

Backing for part 2   Backing for both parts

Flying Without Wings

Words and Music by
Steve Mac and Wayne Hector

Demonstration   Backing for part 1

How Do I Live

Backing for part 2   Backing for both parts

Words and Music by Diane Warren

Demonstration

Backing for part 1

My Heart Will Go On

Backing for part 2

Backing for
both parts

Music by James Horner

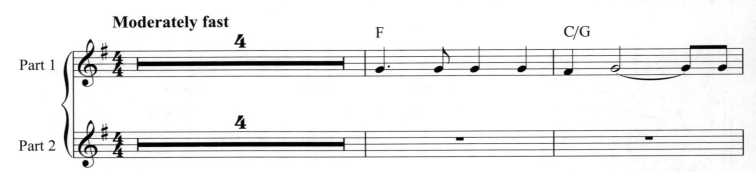

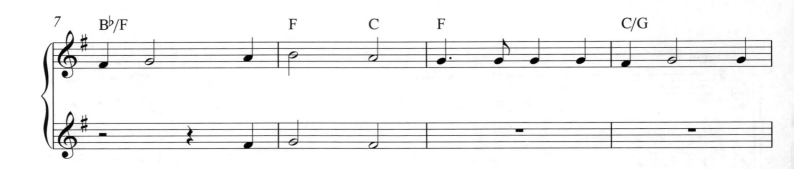

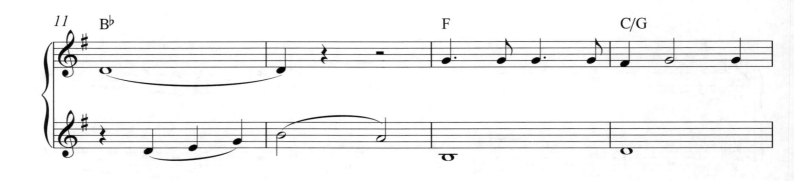

18

Demonstration

Backing for part 1

More Than Words

Backing for part 2

Backing for both parts

Words and Music by
Nuno Bettencourt and Gary Cherone

Demonstration

Backing for part 1

When You Say Nothing At All

Backing for part 2

Backing for both parts

Words and Music by
Paul Overstreet and Don Schlitz

Demonstration   Backing for part 1

You Needed Me

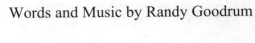
Backing for part 2   Backing for both parts

Words and Music by Randy Goodrum

You can be the featured soloist with
TAKE **THE** LEAD

Collect these titles, each with demonstration and full backing tracks on CD.

90s Hits	Movie Hits	TV Themes	Christmas Songs	The Blues Brothers
The Air That I Breathe (Simply Red)	**Because You Loved Me** (Up Close And Personal)	**Coronation Street**	**The Christmas Song** (Chestnuts Roasting On An Open Fire)	**She Caught The Katy And Left Me A Mule To Ride**
Angels (Robbie Williams)	**Blue Monday** (The Wedding Singer)	**I'll Be There For You** (theme from *Friends*)	**Frosty The Snowman**	**Gimme Some Lovin'**
How Do I Live (LeAnn Rimes)	**(Everything I Do) I Do It For You** (Robin Hood: Prince Of Thieves)	**Match Of The Day**	**Have Yourself A Merry Little Christmas**	**Shake A Tail Feather**
I Don't Want To Miss A Thing (Aerosmith)	**I Don't Want To Miss A Thing** (Armageddon)	**(Meet) The Flintstones**	**Little Donkey**	**Everybody Needs Somebody To Love**
I'll Be There For You (The Rembrandts)	**I Will Always Love You** (The Bodyguard)	**Men Behaving Badly**	**Rudolph The Red-Nosed Reindeer**	**The Old Landmark**
My Heart Will Go On (Celine Dion)	**Star Wars (Main Title)** (Star Wars)	**Peak Practice**	**Santa Claus Is Comin' To Town**	**Think**
Something About The Way You Look Tonight (Elton John)	**The Wind Beneath My Wings** (Beaches)	**The Simpsons**	**Sleigh Ride**	**Minnie The Moocher**
Frozen (Madonna)	**You Can Leave Your Hat On** (The Full Monty)	**The X-Files**	**Winter Wonderland**	**Sweet Home Chicago**
Order ref: 6725A – Flute	Order ref: 6908A – Flute	Order ref: 7003A – Flute	Order ref: 7022A – Flute	Order ref: 7079A - Flute
Order ref: 6726A – Clarinet	Order ref: 6909A – Clarinet	Order ref: 7004A – Clarinet	Order ref: 7023A – Clarinet	Order ref: 7080A – Clarinet
Order ref: 6727A – Alto Saxophone	Order ref: 6910A – Alto Saxophone	Order ref: 7005A – Alto Saxophone	Order ref: 7024A – Alto Saxophone	Order ref: 7081A - Alto Saxophone
Order ref: 6728A – Violin	Order ref: 6911A –Tenor Saxophone	Order ref: 7006A – Violin	Order ref: 7025A – Violin	Order ref: 7082A - Tenor Saxophone
	Order ref: 6912A – Violin		Order ref: 7026A – Piano	Order ref: 7083A - Trumpet
			Order ref: 7027A – Drums	Order ref: 7084A - Violin